Published simultaneously in 2006 by Helen Exley Giftbooks in Great Britain and the USA.

12 11 10 9 8 7 6 5 4 3 2 1

Selection and arrangement copyright © Helen Exley 2006.

The moral right of the author has been asserted.

ISBN 10: 1-84634-033-0

ISBN 13: 1-978-1-84634-033-8

A copy of the CIP data is available from the Brtish Library on request. All rights reserved.

No part of this publication may be reproduced or transmitted in any form or by any means, electronic or otherwise, without permission in writing from the publisher.

Words and pictures selected by Helen Exley.

Printed in China.

Helen Exley Giftbooks, 16 Chalk Hill, Watford, WD19 4BG, UK.

Helen Exley Giftbooks LLC, 185 Main Street, Spencer, MA 01562, USA.

LOVE FOR OUR TIMES

A HELEN EXLEY GIFTBOOK

Nothing is higher
than love

Nothing is sweeter than love;
nothing stronger, nothing higher, nothing wider;
nothing happier, nothing fuller,
nothing better in heaven and earth....

THOMAS À KEMPIS (1380-1471)

LOVE CHANGES THINGS; IT IS THE MOST POWERFUL FORCE IN THE WORLD. A PERSON MOTIVATED BY LOVE IS THE MOST POTENT FORCE THERE IS. THERE ARE OTHER FORCES THAT ARE POTENT, SUCH AS HATRED. BUT LOVE IS A GREATER FORCE.

MILLARD FULLER, FROM "A HOUSE EVERY FIFTY MINUTES"

Love flies, runs and leaps for joy.

It is free and unrestrained.

Love knows no limits, but ardently transcends all bounds.

Love feels no burden, takes no account of toil,

Attempts things beyond its strength.

THOMAS À KEMPIS (1379-1471), FROM "THE IMITATION OF CHRIST"

Infinite love is a weapon of matchless potency.
It is the "summum bonum" of Life.
It is an attribute of the brave, in fact it is their all.
It does not come within the reach of the coward.
It is no wooden or lifeless dogma
but a living and life-giving force.
It is the special attribute of the heart.

MAHATMA GANDHI (1869-1948)

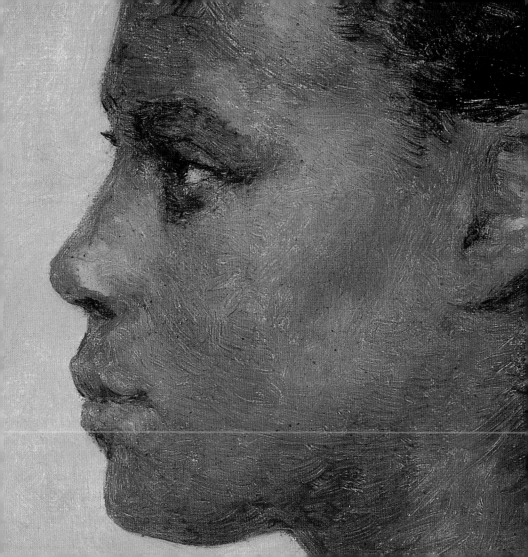

Life is to be fortified by many friendships.
To love and to be loved
is the greatest happiness in existence.

SYDNEY SMITH (1171-1845)

CARE

MONEY IS USEFUL, BUT THE LOVE,
THE ATTENTION, AND THE CARE
WE OFFER TO OTHERS
ARE THE MOST IMPORTANT THINGS.

MOTHER TERESA (1910-1997), FROM "A LIFE FOR GOD"

TOGETHER

Without the human community one single human being cannot survive.

THE DALAI LAMA, B.1935

Love alone

Love alone is capable of uniting living beings
in such a way as to complete and fulfil them,
for it alone takes them and joins them by what
is deepest in themselves.

PIERRE TEILHARD DE CHARDIN (1881-1955)

If we have no peace,
it is because we have forgotten
that we belong to each other.

MOTHER TERESA (1910-1997)

Love... will put its hook into your heart and force you to know that of all strong things nothing is so strong, so irresistible, as love.

WILLIAM LAW (1686-1761)

There is only one element in life
which is worth having at any cost,
and it is love. Love immense and infinite,
broad as the sky and deep as the ocean —
this is the one great gain in life.
Blessed is he who gets it.

SWAMI VIVEKANANDA (1862-1902),
FROM "THE COMPLETE WORKS OF SWAMI VIVEKANANDA" VOL. V

To love is the great Amulet that makes this world a garden.

ROBERT LOUIS STEVENSON (1850-1894)

Love makes bitter things sweet;
love converts base copper to gold.
By love dregs become clear;
by love pains become healing.
By love the dead are brought to life;
by love a king is made a slave.

JALAL AL-DIN RUMI (1207-1273)

One word frees us of all the weight
and pain of life: That word is love.

SOPHOCLES (496-406 B.C.),
FROM "OEDIPUS AT COLONNUS"

Hate cannot destroy hate, but love
can and does... love that suffers
all things and is kind, love that accepts
responsibility, love that marches,
love that suffers, love that bleeds and dies
for a great cause – but to rise again.

DANIEL A. POLING

No one is born hating another person
because of the colour of his skin, or his background,
or his religion. People must learn to hate,
and if they can learn to hate, they can be taught
to love, for love comes more naturally
to the human heart than its opposite.

NELSON MANDELA, B.1918,
FROM "LONG WALK TO FREEDOM"

Melt their

Melt their weapons, melt their hearts,
melt their anger with love.

SHIRLEY MACLAINE, B.1934

anger

It is love that fashions us into the fullness
of our being – not our looks, not our work,
not our wants, not our achievements,
not our parents, not our status, not our dreams.
These are all the fodder and the filler,
the navigating fuels of our lives; but it is love:
who we love, how we love, why we love
and that we love which ultimately shapes us.

DAPHNE ROSE KINGMA

The glory of life,
Is to love, not to be loved,
To serve, not to be served,
To be a strong hand in the dark
To another in the time of need,
To be a cup of strength to any soul
In a crisis of weakness.
This is to know the glory of life.

ARCHBISHOP MICHAEL RAMSEY (1904-1988)

To awaken each morning with a smile brightening my face; to greet the day with reverence for the opportunities it contains; to approach my work with a clean mind; to hold ever before me, even in the doing of little things, the ultimate purpose toward which I am working; to meet men and women with laughter on my lips and love in my heart; to be gentle, kind, and courteous through all the hours; to approach the night with weariness that ever woos sleep and the joy that comes from work well done – this is how I desire to waste wisely my days.

THOMAS DEKKER (C.1570-C.1641)

Bound
together

The world is bound together by acts
of unselfish kindness.

STUART AND LINDA MACFARLANE

The law of love

It is the law of love that rules mankind.
Had violence, i.e. hate, ruled us
we should have become extinct long ago.
And yet, the tragedy of it
is that the so-called civilized men and nations
conduct themselves as if
the basis of society was violence.

MAHATMA GANDHI (1869-1948)

Indifference is the invincible

giant of the world.

OUIDA (1839-1908)

We can cure physical diseases
with medicine but the only cure
for loneliness, despair and hopelessness
is love. There are many in the world
who are dying for a piece of bread
but there are many more dying for
a little love.

MOTHER TERESA (1910-1997), FROM "A SIMPLE PATH"

Nothing on earth is as feeble
and frightened as man, and nothing more
deserving of compassion, of charity.

RONAN BENNETT, FROM "HAVOC IN ITS THIRD YEAR"

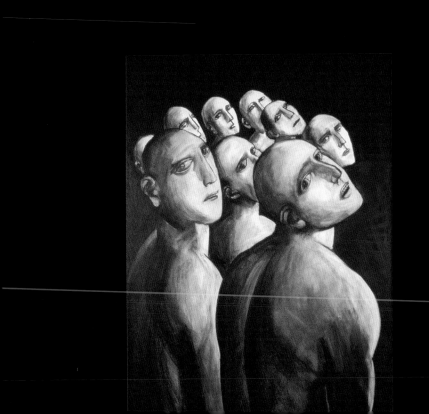

HARMONY

...one of the attributes of love
is to bring harmony
and order out of chaos,
to introduce meaning and effect
where before there was none.

MOLLY HASKELL, B.1940

We need each other to share
the mysteries of life and death,
to give substance to our joy and sorrows,
to help us on our journey,
and to remind us that we are all one.

AUTHOR UNKNOWN

Love is the strongest force the world possesses, and yet it is the humblest imaginable.

MAHATMA GANDHI (1869-1948)

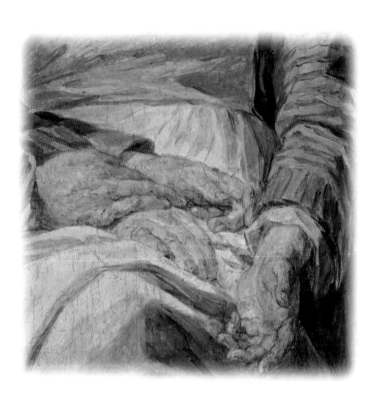

If I treat you as compassionately
as I treat myself – forgiving,
accepting, loving, supporting,
imposing no demands or expectations –
then it's not what I want or expect
that will happen, but something much
more wonderful.

MIKE STRONG

Love from one being to another
can only be that two solitudes come nearer,
recognise and protect and comfort
each other.

H A N   S U Y I N

Love is a great thing, a great good in every way;
it alone lightens what is heavy, and leads smoothly
over all roughness. For it carries a burden without
being burdened, and makes every bitter thing
sweet and tasty. Love wants to be lifted up, not
held back by anything low. Love wants to be free,
and far from all worldly desires, so that its inner
vision may not be dimmed and good fortune bind
it or misfortune cast it down. Nothing is sweeter
than love....

THOMAS À KEMPIS (1379-1471),
FROM "THE IMITATION OF CHRIST"

Love is something like the clouds
that were in the sky before the sun came out.
You cannot touch the clouds, you know;
but you feel the rain and know how glad the flowers
and the thirsty earth are to have it after a hot day.
You cannot touch love either;
but you feel the sweetness that it pours into everything.

ANNIE SULLIVAN (1866-1936)

We need to be loved. We need people to tell us
that we are special and irreplaceable,
people who will tend to our needs,
and banish our fears and insecurities
the way our mothers did when we were infants.
But we also need to give love;
to make a difference in someone's life.

RABBI HAROLD S. KUSHNER

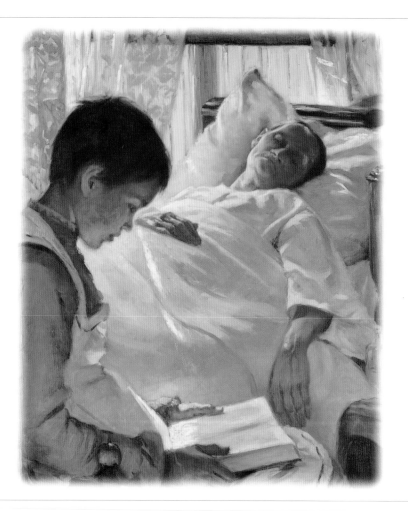

For others...

Do ordinary things
with extraordinary love: little things
like caring for the sick
and the homeless, the lonely
and the unwanted,
washing and cleaning for them.

MOTHER TERESA (1910-1997), FROM "A SIMPLE PATH"

We need no bombs or weapons.
Love is our weapon: love toward the lepers,
the elderly, the dying, the paralytic;
toward all those who have no one and are loved
by no one.

MOTHER TERESA (1910-1997), FROM "HEART OF JOY"

We can know peace

THE CERTAINTY OF LOVE

HOLDS OFF THE FEAR OF ALL CATASTROPHE.

LOVE OUTWEIGHS ALL ELSE

AND WE CAN KNOW PEACE

AT THE HEART OF TUMULT.

PAM BROWN, B.1928

friendship

I said "friendship is the greatest bond in the world",
and I had reason for it,
for it is all the bands that this world hath.

BISHOP JEREMY TAYLOR (1613-1667),
FROM "OF THE NATURE AND OFFICES OF FRIENDSHIP"

When indeed shall we learn
that we are all related one to the other,
that we are all members of one body?
Until the spirit of love for our fellows,
regardless of race, or creed,
shall fill the world, – until the great mass
of the people shall be filled with the sense
of responsibility for each other's welfare,
social justice can never be attained.

HELEN KELLER (1880-1968)

Love courses through everything.
No, love is everything.
How can you say, there is no love,
when nothing but love exists?
All that you see has appeared because of love,
All shines from love,
All pulses from love,
All flows from love —
No, once again all is love.

FARHRUDDIN ARAQI

NO-ONE WHO HAS EVER
BROUGHT UP A CHILD CAN DOUBT
FOR A MOMENT THAT LOVE IS LITERALLY
THE LIFE-GIVING FLUID
OF HUMAN EXISTENCE.

DR. SMILEY BLANTON

greetings

[Love is] all that matters.
Not as some vague romantic concept
but the laughter in the greeting embrace
at the door, and the beans-and-bones
reality of the smell from the stew
on the stove beyond.

NICHOLAS LUARD, FROM "THE FIELD OF THE STAR"

Love is not getting, but giving.
Not a wild dream of pleasure and a madness
of desire – oh, no – love is not that!
It is goodness and honour and peace and pure living –
yes, love is that and it is the best thing
in the world and the thing that lives the longest.

HENRY VAN DYKE (1852-1933)

It is in the shelter of each other
that the people live.

IRISH PROVERB

Disasters sweep the world – war and disease,
earthquake and flood and fire –
but always in their wake come acts of courage
and concern that astound the human heart.
Light in utter darkness.

CHARLOTTE GRAY, B.1937

DISASTERS

A child's

need

We try to give our children
everything
— when all they need is love
and certainty.

PAM BROWN, B.1928

We watch the news. The strutting generals,
the shrieking demagogues, the ranting politicians
with an axe to grind, the bigots and the brainwashed.
The prisoners with empty eyes.
The wounded soldiers. The fathers weeping
for lost families. And those who work to mend
the torn societies, the ruined lives,
the wounds. All someone's sons.
Remember them. They are all your brothers.

PAM BROWN, B.1928

I believe that the sum total of the energy
of mankind is not to bring us down but to lift us up,
and that this is the result of the definite,
if unconscious, working of the law of love.
The fact that mankind persists shows that the
cohesive force is greater than the disruptive force
centripetal force greater than centrifugal.

MAHATMA GANDHI (1869-1948), FROM "YOUNG INDIA"

...forever

There is a love like a small lamp, which goes out
when the oil is consumed; or like a stream
which dries up when it doesn't rain.
But there is a love that is like a mighty spring
gushing up out of the earth; it keeps flowing forever,
and is inexhaustible.

ISAAC OF NINEVEH

The fullness of our heart is expressed
in the way we receive, in the way we need,
in the way we touch, in everything
that we write and say, in the way we walk,
and in what others see in our eyes.

MOTHER TERESA (1910-1997)

I think that the most significant work we ever do,
in our whole world, in our whole life,
is done within the four walls of our own home.
All mothers and fathers, whatever their stations
in life, can make the most significant
of contributions by imprinting the spirit of service
on the souls of their children,
so that the children grow up committed to making
a difference.

STEPHEN R. COVEY, PH.D.

...and

courage comes

When the heart sinks to despair, we remember those
who enfold the sufferers in love, who build them shelters,
find them food, heal their wounds and their diseases.
Contact the bereaved. Are mothers to the children.
Give hope of a new beginning. Out of horror comes
courage beyond belief. Given only a little,
children learn to laugh again —
and to give to those who care for them
a joy that cancels every difficulty they have endured.

PAM BROWN, B.1928

Everybody can be great. Because everybody can serve.
You don't have to have a college degree to serve.
You don't have to make your subject and your verb
agree to serve. You don't have to know about Plato
and Aristotle to serve. You don't have to know
Einstein's theory of relativity to serve. You don't have
to know the second theory of thermodynamics in
physics to serve. You only need a heart full of grace.
A soul generated by love.

MARTIN LUTHER KING, JR (1929-1968)

There is only one real deprivation,
I decided this morning,
and that is not to be able to give one's gifts
to those one loves most.

MAY SARTON (1912-1995)

deprivation

TWO BROTHERS

Two brothers worked together on the family farm.
One was married and had a large family. The other
was single. At the day's end, the brothers shared
everything equally, produce and profit.

Then one day the single brother said to himself,
"It's not right that we should share equally the produce
and the profit. I'm alone and my needs are simple."
So each night he took a sack of grain from his bin
and crept across the field between their houses,
dumping it into his brother's bin.

Meanwhile, the married brother said to himself,
"It's not right that we should share the produce and
the profit equally. After all, I'm married and I have my
wife and children to look after me in years to come.

My brother has no one, and no one to take care of his future." So each night he took a sack of grain and dumped it into his single brother's bin.

Both men were puzzled for years because their supply of grain never dwindled. Then one dark night the two brothers bumped into each other. Slowly it dawned on them what was happening. They dropped their sacks and embraced one another.

AUTHOR UNKNOWN,
FROM "MORE SOWER'S SEEDS" BY BRIAN CAVANAUGH

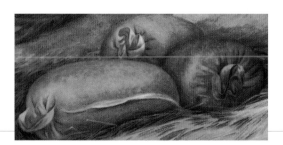

Somewhere in the inner darkness of our minds
lie the recollections of those others, the children,
blown away like a flurry of leaves by sickness,
sorrow and devilry, by hunger and by war.

PAM BROWN, B.1928

Each sorrow and each joy is universal.
These seeming strangers are your family.

PAM BROWN, B.1928

I am done with great things and big plans,
great institutions and big success. I am for those tiny,
invisible loving human forces that work from individual
to individual, creeping through the crannies
of the world like so many rootlets,
or like the capillary oozing of water, which, if given time,
will rend the hardest monuments of pride.

WILLIAM JAMES (1842-1910)

We can do no great things – only small things with great love.

MOTHER TERESA (1910-1997)

All the world is searching for joy
and happiness, but these cannot
be purchased for any price
in any marketplace, because
they are virtues that come from
within, and like rare jewels
must be polished,
for they shine brightest...
in the services of brotherly love.

LUCILLE R. TAYLOR

Not for any price

THE SOURCE OF LOVE IS DEEP IN US AND WE CAN HELP
OTHERS REALIZE A LOT OF HAPPINESS.
ONE WORD, ONE ACTION, ONE THOUGHT CAN REDUCE
ANOTHER PERSON'S SUFFERING
AND BRING THAT PERSON JOY.

THICH NHAT HANH, B.1926

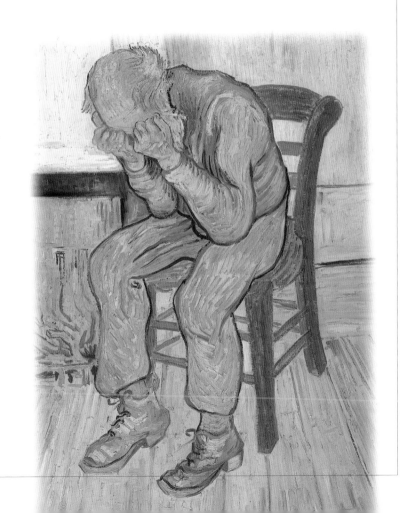

among the
outcasts

...in the gentle relief of another's care,

in the darkness of night and the winter's snow;

in the naked and outcast – seek love there.

WILLIAM BLAKE (1757-1827)

MOTHER COURAGE

In the wake of every evil inflicted by man or nature
come the women, gathering what can be salvaged,
the distraught and injured children, the lost,
the dispossessed, the fragments of a broken society.
They stoop across every battlefield,
seeking for their own. They tear at blocks of stone
tumbled by earthquake, blackened by fire.
They build among the olive trees or the desert sand.

PAM BROWN, B.1928

The sole valid foundation for universal responsibility is love and compassion. Love and compassion are the ultimate source of joy and happiness.
Once we recognise their value and actually try to cultivate them, many other good qualities – forgiveness, tolerance, inner strength and confidence to overcome fear and insecurity – come forth naturally. These qualities are essential if we are to create a better, happier, more stable and civilised world.

HIS HOLINESS THE DALAI LAMA

Familiar acts are beautiful through love.

PERCY BYSSHE SHELLEY (1792-1822),
FROM "PROMETHEUS UNBOUND"

IT IS NOT THE PERFECT, BUT THE IMPERFECT, WHO HAVE NEED OF LOVE.

OSCAR WILDE (1854-1900)

Little do people perceive what solitude is,
and how far it extendeth.
For a crowd is not company, and faces
are but a gallery of pictures, and talk
but a tinkling cymbal, where there is no love.

FRANCIS BACON (1561-1626)

We accept responsibility for those
who stare at photographers from behind
barbed wire, who can't bound down the street
in a new pair of sneakers, who were born
in places we wouldn't be caught dead,
who never go to the circus,
who live in an X-rated world.

And we accept responsibility for
those who never get dessert,
who have no safe blanket to drag behind them,
who watch their parents watch them die,
who can't find any bread to steal,
who don't have any rooms to clean up,
whose pictures aren't on anybody's dresser,
and whose monsters are real.

INA J. HUGHES, EXTRACT FROM "PRAYER FOR CHILDREN"

beauty

The stars dwarf our little sun.
We are lost at the edges of
one little galaxy.
And yet we possess beauty, pity,
kindliness and love.
And so outshine the stars.

PAM BROWN, B.1928

Out of destruction the women piece together
small areas of safety, letting fragments stand as symbols
of a whole. Here is a house, patched out of cardboard;
here is a kitchen, stocked with rusted cans.
Here is a cradle in a nest of rags. The earth erupts,
the typhoon sweeps away a clutch of villages,
the causes rage across the landscape,
the bitter wire divides. But the women crouch
beside their fires and hide the children in their shawls.
They have suffered too much in making life
to let it go so easily; they cannot think in cold statistics
or see the death of any child as a necessity.

PAM BROWN, B.1928

It isn't difficult to see how the world today, its beauty and grandeur notwithstanding, the conquests of science and technology notwithstanding, the sought-after and abounding material goods it has to offer notwithstanding, is thirsty for more truth, more love, more joy.

HIS HOLINESS POPE JOHN PAUL II (1920-2005), FROM "AGENDA FOR THE THIRD MILLENNIUM"

Loving kindness is greater than laws....

THE TALMUD

The subject of love is exhaustible. In that little word
is hidden the key to our own happiness as well
as to the survival of the world.
While modern culture has generated oceans
of information, we are rarely the wiser for it.
Information is not our greatest need; opening our hearts
to the creative and life-giving spirit of love is.

ELIZABETH ROBERTS & ELIAS AMIDON,
FROM "PRAYERS FOR A THOUSAND YEARS"

HOLD TIGHTLY TO POSSESSIONS.
HOLD TIGHTLY TO FRIENDSHIP.
HOLD GENTLY TO LOVE.

PAM BROWN, B.1928

For finally, we are as we love.
It is love that measures our stature.

WILLIAM SLOANE COFFIN (1877-1954)

LOVE ALWAYS FINDS ITS WAY
TO AN IMPRISONED SOUL,
AND LEADS IT OUT INTO THE WORLD OF
FREEDOM AND INTELLIGENCE!

HELEN KELLER (1880-1968)

imprisoned

It is a terrible thing, this kindness
that human beings do not lose.
Terrible because when we are
finally naked in the dark and cold,
it is all we have. We who are
so rich, so full of strength, wind
up with that small change.
We have nothing else to give.

URSULA K. LE GUIN, B.1929

"Love him? There is nothing left to love."
"There is always something left to love.
And if you ain't learned that,
you ain't learned nothing.
Have you cried for that boy today?...
What he been through and what it done to him.
Child, when do you think is the time to love
somebody the most; when they done good
and made things easy for everybody?
Well then, you ain't through learning –
because that ain't the time at all.
It's when he's at his lowest and can't
believe in hisself 'cause the world done
whipped him so...."

LORRAINE HANSBERRY (1930-1965),
FROM "A RAISIN IN THE SUN"

I understand

All, everything that I understand,
I understand only because I love.

LEO TOLSTOY (1828-1910)

The last piece

of bread

We who lived in concentration camps
can remember the men who walked through
the huts comforting others,
giving away their last piece of bread.
They may have been few in number, but they offer
sufficient proof that everything can be taken away
from a man but one thing:
the last of the human freedoms — to choose one's
attitude in any given set of circumstances,
to choose one's own way.

VIKTOR FRANKL

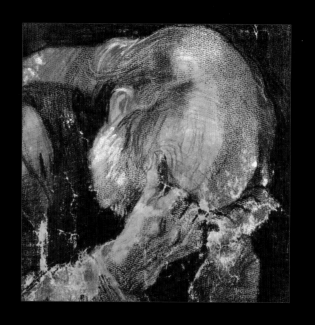

There are so many sorrows in today's world!
These sorrows are due to hunger,
to dislodging, to all kinds of illnesses.
I am convinced that the greatest
of all sorrows is to feel alone,
to feel unwanted, deprived of all affection.
It consists in not having anyone,
in having gotten to the point of forgetting
what human contact is,
what human love is, what it means
to be wanted, to be loved, to have a family....
May we all be instruments of peace, of love,
and of compassion.

MOTHER TERESA (1910-1997), FROM "HEART OF JOY"

Every year and every hour of my life
has been a time of love.
Every friend, every neighbour, and even
enemy, have been the messengers
and instruments of love.
Every state and change of my life,
notwithstanding my sin, have opened to me
the treasures and mysteries of love.

RICHARD BAXTER (1615-1691)

LEARN TO LIVE

You live that you may learn to love.
You love that you may learn to live.
No other lesson is required of us.

MIKHAIL NAIMY (1889-1988), FROM
"THE BOOK OF MIRDAD"

This is what sets this tiny opal of a planet
off from a million greater worlds
— the possibility of kindness
— the possibility of care.
Love transforms it into a place of wonder.

PAM BROWN, B.1928

Some day, after we have mastered
the winds, the waves, the tides
and gravity we shall harness
the energies of love.
Then, for the second time
in the history of the world,
man will have discovered fire.

PIERRE TEILHARD DE CHARDIN (1881-1955)

...without end

Love knows no limits to its endurance,
no end to its trust, no dashing of its hope;
it can outlast anything.
It is, in fact the one thing that still
stands when all else has fallen.

ADAPTED FROM I CORINTHIANS 13:1-2, 4-7

CIRCLES

Love is the vital essence that pervades
and permeates from the centre
of the circumference, the graduating circles
of all thought and action.
Love is the talisman of human weal
and woe – the open sesame to every soul.

ELIZABETH CADY STANTON (1815-1902)

Love is over all

Time flies, suns rise,
and shadows fall –
Let them go by, for love is over all.

FOUND ON A SUNDIAL

ACKNOWLEDGEMENTS
The publishers are grateful for permission to reproduce copyright material. Whilst every effort has been made to trace copyright holders, the publishers would be pleased to hear from any not here acknowledged.

MARILYN FERGUSON: From *The Aquarian Conspiracy*, published by Jeremy P. Tarcher/Putnam.

VIKTOR FRANKL: From *Man's Search for Meaning*. Used with permission from The Random House Group Ltd and Beacon Press.

THICH NHAT HANH: From *Teachings on Love*, published by Parallax Press.

LORRAINE HANSBURY: From *A Raisin in the Sun*. Used with permission from Random House, Inc.

THOMAS À KEMPIS: From *Into the Garden*, published by HarperCollins.

DAPHNE ROSE KINGMA: Excerpted from *365 Days of Love (formerly Garland of Love)* by Daphne Rose Kingma, with permission of Conari Press, imprint of Red Wheel/Weiser, MA and San Francisco, CA. To order please call 1-800-423-7087.

NELSON MANDELA: From *Long Walk to Freedom*, published by Hachette Book Group.

POPE JOHN PAUL II: Taken from *Agenda for the third Millennium*, by Pope John Paul II, published by Zondervan.

CATHERINE PONDER: From *The Dynamic Laws of Prosperity*, published by DeVorss & Company.

MOTHER TERESA: Taken from *Heart of Joy*, published by Zondervan.

MOTHER TERESA: From *The Simple Path*, published by Ballantine Books and Random House.

Important copyright notice:
Pam Brown, Charlotte Gray, Stuart & Linda Macfarlane are © Helen Exley 2006.

LIST OF ILLUSTRATIONS
Helen Exley Giftbooks would like to thank the following organizations and individuals for permission to reproduce their pictures:
AKG-Images (AKG); The Bridgeman Art Library (BAL), Edimedia (EDM); The Fine Art Photographic Library (FAP); Scala; Superstock; Topfoto. Whilst every reasonable effort has been made to trace copyright holders, the publishers would be pleased to hear from the any not here acknowledged.

Page 40: Title and artist unknown
Page 47: Artist unknown, private collection
The publishers have been unable to trace the copyright holders for these pictures and would be grateful if the representatives for these artists could contact them.

Front Cover, Title Page, pages 6, 28: *The Rising Sun*, GIUSEPPE PELIZZA DA VOLPEDO, Nazione d'Arte Moderna, Rome, Italy/BAL

Page 8: *Rice Winnowing*, © FERNANDO C. AMORSOLO, 2006

Page 10: *Dance*, 1996, FRANCKS DECEUS (contemporary artist), private collection/BAL

Page 13: *Young Negress*, FERNAND CORMON, Musee des Beaux-Arts, Pau, France/ Giraudon/BAL

Page 15: *Playground, Lesbos*, 1996, ANDREW MACARA (contemporary artist), private collection/ BAL

Page 17: *Cupid and Psyche*, SIR EDWARD BURNES-JONES (1833-1898) © Sheffield Galleries and Museums Trust, UK/BAL

Page 19: *Return from Fishing with Setting Sun*, Eugene Boudin, Musee d'Art Thomas Henry, Cherbourg/BAL

Page 21: *The Harvester's Supper*, 1898, HENRY HERBERT LA THANGUE (1859-1929) © Bradford Art Galleries and Museums, West Yorkshire, UK/BAL

Page 22: *Les Haleurs de la Volga*, EUGENE REPINE (1870-73), Russian Museum, St Petersburg/BAL

Page 24: *The Sisters*, EMILE CLAUS (1849-1942), FAP

Page 27: *Ripe Wheatfields*, AUGUST (FRITZ) OVERBECK (1869-1909). Worpsweder Kunsthalle, Stade, Germany/BAL

Page 31: *Dancing Partner 1991*, © BENCAB, 2006

Page 33: *Job* (oil on canvas), LEON JOSEPH FLORENTIN BONNART (1833-1922), Musee Bonnat, Bayonne, France/Lauros/Giraudon/BAL

Page 34: *In Detention*, 1888, AUGUSTE JOSEPH TRUPHEME (1836-98), Musee de la Ville de Paris, Musee du Petit-Palais, France/Lauros/Giraudon/BAL

Page 37: *Tell Al-Zaater, 1976, In Shelter*, ISMAIL SHAMMOUT, EDM

Page 38: *Buy a Bunch of Pretty Flowers?*, 1883, GEORGE MORTON (fl.1879-1904), private Collection/Manya Igel Fine Arts Ltd., London, UK/BAL

Page 43: *Breakfast Table*, JOSEPH MILNER KITE (1862-1946), Waterhouse and Dodd, London, UK/BAL

Page 44: *In the Rain*, 1882 VINCENT VAN GOGH (1853-90), Haags Gemeentemuseum, The Hague, Netherlands/BAL

Page 49: © 2006 Peter Kettle

Page 51: *Man Leaning on a Parapet*, GEORGES PIERRE SEURAT (1859-1891), private Collection/BAL

Page 53: *Looking Back*, 1984 (charcoal on paper) EVELYN WILLIAMS (Contemporary Artist), private collection/BAL

Page 54: *Estate in New England*, 1912, MAURICE PRENDERGAST (1859-1924), Washington DC, Smithsonian American Art Museum © 2005, Foto Smithsonian American Art Museum/Art Resource/Scala, Firenze

Page 57: *Three Girls*, AMRITA SHER-GIL, private collection

Pages 58/59: *Children and Young Girls picking Flowers in a Meadow North of Skagen*, MICHAEL PETER ANCHER (1849-1927) Skagens Museum, Denmark/BAL

Page 60: *The Agreed Proposal* (oil on panel) NICHOLAS-BERNARD LEPICIE (1735-1784) Musee d'Art Thomas Henry, Cherbourg, France/Giraudon/BAL

Page 62: *The Companions, 1909*, ERNEST WAELVERT (1880-1946), private Collection/© Whitford & Hughes, London, UK/BAL

Page 65: *Lunchtime Preparations*, WILLIAM KAY BLACKLOCK, FAP